WHY I LOVE GRANDPA

Other books by Gregory E. Lang:

Why a Daughter Needs a Dad

Why a Son Needs a Dad

Why I Love Grandma

WHY I LOVE GRANDPA

100 reasons

GREGORY E. LANG

with Meagan Lang

Cumberland House
Nashville, Tennessee

Published by
    Cumberland House Publishing, Inc.
    431 Harding Industrial Drive
    Nashville, TN 37211

Cover design: Unlikely Suburban Design
Text design: Lisa Taylor

Library of Congress Cataloging-in-Publication Data

Lang, Gregory E., 1960–
    Why I love grandpa: 100 reasons / Gregory E. Lang with Meagan Lang.
        p. cm.
    ISBN 1-58182-360-6
    1. Grandfathers—Miscellanea. 2. Grandparent and child—Miscellanea. I. Lang, Meagan, 1990– II. Title.
    HQ759.9.L343 2003
    306.874'5—dc21

2003012618

Printed in the United States of America
1 2 3 4 5 6 7 8 — 08 07 06 05 04 03

Dedicated with love to Jacobs Eugene Lang

and in memory of

Obie Lee "O. L." Brown
Charles Miller Lang
Howard Eugene "Gene" Hord

⚜

To Gramps—for many fond memories of love, laughs,
and good times. You mean the world to me.

—Meagan

Introduction

Prominent in my home is a handsome dining table made of heart of pine. Large enough to comfortably seat ten adults, it is affectionately referred to as the "Table of Hearts." My grandfather made it for my mother more than thirty-five years ago, and she gave it to me. Built of salvaged wood, its top surface hand planed to a smooth finish and its legs hand turned from one of his patterns, the table is a daily reminder to me of my grandfather, Obie Lee "O. L." Brown, master craftsman, father of seven, and grandfather to twenty-two.

My grandfather was a major figure in my early years, and although he died before I became a teenager, I carry his beloved memory with me still. Along with my parents, he is credited with shaping the man I have become, and along with my father is the model for the grandfather I hope to be one day.

O. L. Brown was a self-taught maker of fine furniture. As a young boy I sat at his feet many an evening to watch *Gunsmoke* or *The Red Skelton Show*, at his side as he drove the pickup truck to the hardware store, or across the table from him on Saturday mornings while we enjoyed a cup of coffee, mine mostly milk, and a bowl of cold cereal. When finished with breakfast we walked across the back yard to his woodshop, where we stayed busy for hours until Grandmomma brought out ham sandwiches and sweet iced tea for lunch. I was too young to help much, except for moving boards from one stack to another or sweeping sawdust. He died when I was twelve. My eyes still water when I think about him, especially on Sunday mornings as I drink coffee from what was his favorite mug, now one of my most prized possessions.

O. L. was a tall, barrel-chested man who wore his hair cut close to his head and nearly always dressed in overalls, complete with a finely sharpened pencil in his pocket "just in case." He made funny faces, played practical jokes, and carried candy in his pockets at all times. I remember many stories about his childhood and our family history, stories he told me while sitting on the front porch, or on afternoon rides into the country to see old houses where relatives once lived or churches once attended. I remember his desire to work and make things with his hands, both of which he did until he was in his early seventies, and his pride when giving a just-finished piece of furniture to one of his children or grandchildren. I remember how he would drive for hours to attend the homecoming picnics held at the old family cemetery, where we cleaned, weeded, and repaired family plots under the hot Georgia sun before sitting in the shade of ancient oak trees to enjoy a fine lunch prepared by the women of the family. It is there where he was laid to rest, alongside my grandmother. Today, all these years later, when I find myself driving into south Georgia, I take the short detour off the highway to sit under the old tree in the cemetery and think of these people who were so dear to me.

It was my grandfather who first impressed upon me the importance of family, of tradition, and of loving one's work. These are values that remain with me today, that I try now to impress upon my child. I have placed several photographs of my grandfather around my home and have enjoyed telling my daughter about him when the occasion arises. Like me when I was a young boy, my daughter has only one grandfather to enjoy. I make sure that they have ample time to spend together, so that she is left with as many memories of growing up with him as I have of growing up with O. L.

My child, Meagan Katherine, loves her grandfather with the same intensity that I loved mine. Known to her as "Gramps," he lets her know that she is special to him, and they have a rhythm when interacting together that is all their own. They play, tease, and torment one another with pet names or taunts about embarrassing events of the past. They try to scare each other coming around corners, purposefully get in each other's way, and embrace and kiss at the beginning and end of each visit. She looks at his old photographs and listens with great interest as he tells her about the people within them. He makes things for her, and she enjoys being with him in his shop. He explains to her what he is doing as he restores an old car, and they sit in rocking chairs on the front porch and talk late into the night, or watch television together until one of them falls asleep. Meagan keeps a picture of him and her grandmother on our refrigerator, and she laughs when she tells her friends about the last joke that Gramps played on her.

In my father I see the best qualities of a grown man that make for a wonderful grandfather. He loves his grandchildren unconditionally; he remembers how to have fun; he comes to their aid without hesitation; and he extends a calm patience and understanding that sometimes elude overwhelmed parents.

It was Meagan who first encouraged me to write this book and its companion, *Why I Love Grandma*, as a way to memorialize our love for my parents and Mrs. Ann Hord, her grandparents. Together we made a list of what each of us enjoyed about our grandfathers, and we thought of what we admired most about the many grandfather-grandchild relationships we have witnessed. As she helped me in taking the photographs for this project she was touched by the personal stories that were shared with us, and those stories combined with our own to help us write this book.

With this book Meagan Katherine and I celebrate the grandfathers we love, and recognize them for the many caring gestures that have been extended to us. We also celebrate the wonderful grandfathers we met while creating this book, those who stand in when fathers are absent, who welcome new grandchildren into the family no matter what their origin, who give of themselves unselfishly and continuously, who travel great distances on short notice just because their company has been requested, who share traditions and willingly learn of new ways from young and delighted teachers, who remember their youth and relive it when given the chance to do so, and who speak with a wisdom and understanding that enrich the lives of those who listen. With this book we hope to give grandchildren a special way to reach out to their grandfathers and speak to them of what is in their hearts. At the back of the book there is space for the grandchild to include a family photo and write his or her own one-hundredth reason for loving Grandpa.

My child and I reviewed the first draft of this book while sitting at the Table of Hearts, the dining table that is to be passed on to her when she has a family of her own. She pointed to the many scratches and dents that she as a child made on the table, once banging her fork to get my attention, or working a bit too carelessly on a craft or school project. She asked me if I would ever refinish the table to remove these signs of use. "No," I said. "Granddaddy meant for this table to remind us of what we have done as a family." She then shared with me her favorite memories of family gatherings and other celebrations that have taken place around the Table of Hearts, and I smiled as I nodded in approval and whispered to the memory of O. L., "It does remind us, Granddaddy, it does."

WHY I LOVE GRANDPA

I love Grandpa because

he knows where the really big fish are.

❧

I love Grandpa because

he lets me get away with something now and then.

❧

I love Grandpa because

he makes things for me with his own hands.

❧

I love Grandpa because . . .

he pays me to do chores for him.

he shows me off with pride.

he calls me just to say hello.

he helps me with my school projects.

I love Grandpa because

he doesn't forget I'm just a kid.

I love Grandpa because

he makes each grandchild feel uniquely special.

I love Grandpa because . . .

he knows where the best donuts are made.

he doesn't tease me when I have a crush.

he never loses his patience with me.

he lets me use his tools.

I love Grandpa because

he doesn't sweat the small stuff.

I love Grandpa because

he keeps me laughing.

I love Grandpa because . . .

he understands when I need to be alone.

he helps me see what I cannot
yet see for myself.

he makes room for me in every conversation.

he treats others with dignity.

I love Grandpa because

he lets me drive in the yard.

I love Grandpa because

he always makes time for me.

I love Grandpa because

he does a good deed every day.

I love Grandpa because

he teaches me how to play well with others.

I love Grandpa because . . .

he marvels at my magic tricks.

he encourages me every day.

he likes to drive with the windows down.

he doesn't mind when I act weird.

I love Grandpa because

he gives me straight answers.

I love Grandpa because

he is a safe spot for me to turn to.

I love Grandpa because

he helps me accept what I cannot understand.

I love Grandpa because . . .

he offers guidance when I need it most.

he gives me the courage to face what frightens me.

he shows me how to handle my disputes
with diplomacy.

he is my moral guide.

I love Grandpa because

he teaches me how to play pool.

I love Grandpa because . . .

he plans ahead for my rainy days.

he teaches me to finish the hard work first.

he teaches me to keep my promises.

he shows me that faith is the
strongest foundation.

I love Grandpa because

he listens with interest to everything I say.

I love Grandpa because

he lets me tease him.

I love Grandpa because

he teaches me how to think strategically.

I love Grandpa because

he takes me on weekend adventures.

I love Grandpa because

he dotes on me.

I love Grandpa because

he teaches me about strength of character.

❧

I love Grandpa because . . .

he helps me appreciate the wisdom of elders.

he teaches me about love of country
and pride of community.

he shows me the meaning of loyalty.

he teaches me how to sing the national anthem.

I love Grandpa because

he does not treat me like a child.

I love Grandpa because

he challenges me to be the best I can be.

I love Grandpa because

he will drop everything to help me.

I love Grandpa because

he knows more than anyone else I know.

I love Grandpa because . . .

he gives me his spare change.

he helps me add to my collection.

he is supportive of all that I do.

he is proof that there is a playful child
inside every adult.

I love Grandpa because

he gives advice I can listen to.

I love Grandpa because

he makes me want to be patriotic.

I love Grandpa because

he helps me appreciate our family history.

I love Grandpa because

he understands me.

❧

I love Grandpa because . . .

he teaches me to be grateful for what I have.

he shares with me what took him
years to learn.

he teaches me to love the work that I do.

he teaches me to honor my mate.

I love Grandpa because

he teaches me to contribute generously

as often as I can.

I love Grandpa because

he is proud of everyone in his family.

I love Grandpa because . . .

he always has a peppermint in his pocket.

he teaches me how to dance the twist.

he helps me recognize life's subtle lessons.

he urges me to show others that they are loved.

I love Grandpa because

he smells like cedar and Old Spice.

I love Grandpa because

he tells me about the way things used to be.

I love Grandpa because

he can read my mind.

I love Grandpa because

he cheers louder for me than anyone else.

I love Grandpa because . . .

he teaches me that it is wise to seek advice.

he teaches me to show respect for public servants.

he teaches me to accept the differences in others.

he explains what a woman expects
from a gentleman.

I love Grandpa because

he takes me to the state fair.

I love Grandpa because

he doesn't act his age.

❧

I love Grandpa because . . .

he teaches me to plan ahead.

he shows me how to dance the waltz.

he encourages me to carry my own weight.

he shows me that an old dog
can learn new tricks.

I love Grandpa because

he takes me everywhere he goes.

❧

I love Grandpa because

he has never shown disappointment in me.

❧

I love Grandpa because

he teaches me to appreciate what others do for me.

I love Grandpa because

he thinks I'm funny.

I love Grandpa because

he teaches me that sometimes the best response

is to do nothing.

I love Grandpa because . . .

he knows how to pull off a good practical joke.

he keeps a picture of me with him at all times.

he takes time to help me practice.

he always says the right thing at the right time.

I love Grandpa because . . .

he is patient and wise.

he makes sure we honor our family traditions.

he helps me understand my parents.

he lives by the Golden Rule every day.

I love Grandpa because

he is wonderful, and I want to grow up

to be just like him.

Paste your picture here
and write your reason
on the opposite page.

I love Grandpa because

_____

Acknowledgments

This book could not have been written without the support and generosity of many people. I offer a special thanks to the families who shared their stories with me, who stood in the cold and wet to pose for these photographs, and who indulged me over and over again as I said, "Just one more." Meagan and I were touched by the love we witnessed in the time we spent with you.

I also wish to thank my friend Janet Lankford-Moran, who helped me hide my mistakes and gave me council while I pretended to be a photographer, and the administration of Greater Atlanta Christian school, which helped me recruit families to participate in creating this book.

Finally, I wish to thank Ron Pitkin and his staff at Cumberland House, who have encouraged me and helped me as I worked on this book. Ron, I appreciate your vision and thank you for giving me the venue to touch readers in the way that the books we have done together have. My deepest appreciation and warmest regards always.

To Contact the Authors

write in care of the publisher:
Cumberland House Publishing
431 Harding Industrial Drive
Nashville, TN 37211

or email:
greg.lang@mindspring.com